the Well-Trained Dog

by Elisabeth Schnabel

yearBOOKS,INC.

Dr. Herbert R. Axelrod,
Founder & Chairman

Neal Pronek
Chief Editor

yearBOOKS are all photo
composed, color
separated and designed
on Scitex equipment in
Neptune, N.J. with the
following staff:

GITAL PRE-PRESS
Robert Onyrscuk
Jose Reyes

COMPUTER ART
Thomas J. Ceballos
Patti Escabi
Sandra Taylor Gale
Candida Moreira
Joanne Muzyka
P. Northrup
Francine Shulman

Advertising Sales
George Campbell
Chief
Amy Manning
Director

©yearBOOKS,Inc.
1 TFH Plaza
Neptune, N.J. 07753
Completely manufactured
in Neptune, N.J. USA

Dog training is not limited to teaching good manners and tricks. The most important part of training must be to guide the dog's character development in such a way that he will fit into our way of life without problems.

Dogs, just like people, are mixtures of various character traits, both desirable and undesirable. These traits influence each other, and each dog is different. Even experienced trainers will often find themselves faced with previously unencountered problems. For that reason, there can be no one prescription for dog training success. All we can do is give advice and suggestions that must be applied with regard for the individuality of each trainee.

Understanding instinctive canine behavior assists the trainer in building and maintaining a satisfying relationship with his dog. The trainer who understands his dog will also be able to properly guide the dog's development.

This book is written to advise dog owners who want friendly, temperamentally stable companions with whom they can live without conflict, and who can do justice to their role as protectors of home and hearth.

ORIGINALLY PUBLISHED IN GERMANY BY FRANCKH KOSMOS UNDER THE TITLE *UNSER HUNDWIRD GUT ERZOGEN*, BY ELISABETH SCHNABEL.

What are Quarterlies?

Books, the usual way information of this sort is transmitted, can be too slow. Sometimes by the time a book is written and published, the material contained therein is a year or two old...and no new material has been added during that time. Only a book in a magazine form can bring breaking stories and current information. A magazine is streamlined in production, so we have adopted certain magazine publishing techniques in the creation of this Dog Quarterly. Magazines also can be much cheaper than books because they are supported by advertising. To combine these assets into a great publication, we issued this Quarterly in both magazine and book format at different prices.

Contents

the WORLD from a Dog's Point of View

Realizing that dogs do not think like humans, dog owners must try to communicate in ways that their dogs can understand.

In order to recognize a dog's predisposition, we must look at the qualities that canines inherited from their ancestors the wolves. Some of the following characteristics allow us to draw some conclusions about our dogs' origin as hunters and predators:

- their teeth, with the dangerous carnassials
- their outstanding scenting ability, which surpasses human faculties
- their sensitive hearing, which considerably surpasses human sound and frequency ranges
- their posture - at least that of the large breeds

It is difficult to imagine that a wolf was the ancestor of a cute Pekingese or a bow-legged Dachshund. However, mutations and selection over many millennia serve to explain such enormous differences in size and temperament, just as they explain the kinship between house cat and tiger. If we accept that our dogs are descendants of primeval wolves, we may assume that they still retain in their hereditary make-up a number of wolf-like characteristics, even if only in diluted forms. For example, dogs have no need to go hunting for food, since their "prey" is served to them in their food bowls. Thus, their predator instincts are not used and, thus, have atrophied.

Furthermore, our own clever ancestors adapted the wild wolf to their lifestyle—tamed him, civilized him, domesticated him, and, finally, befriended him. There is no need to be afraid that a "wild wolf" is hiding inside our lovable dog! However, he still retains some characteristics of the wolf, traits that were formed in the ancient communal pack:

- subordination under the authority of the leader
- ability to scent dangers that may threaten the pack
- readiness to defend the pack against enemies

These traits will also be found in our dogs:

- obedience, even devotion, to the pack leader
- watchfulness
- the instinct to defend territory and to protect

When a dog looks up to his owner with trust, the foundation for a happy relationship has been built.

It's difficult to imagine the cuddly puppy or the friendly house pet as the predecessors of the wolf; however, some pack instincts still remain in domesticated dogs.

There are, however, some undesirable primeval instincts preserved in his hereditary make-up; for example, the instinct to pursue and the instinct for aggression toward suspicious or fearful people. These two instincts may be useful for police work and guard duty, but not in our home.

These traits still determine, in part, how dogs behave in the environment that they share with us. A dog's sensory perception also largely determines how he behaves.

Dogs, scientists tell us, hear exponentially better than we do, being able to detect frequencies that lie above our perception range. No doubt dogs experience the world of sounds differently and more intensively than we do. Even further apart are our respective senses of smell. The amount of information a dog gathers through his nose is absolutely astonishing. Dogs

DOG'S POINT OF VIEW

perceive their environment, to a large extent, through their exceedingly sensitive noses. They live in a large world of penetrating scents.

Astonishing—almost bordering on telepathic—is a dog's ability to sense our emotions. He knows immediately who is friend and who is foe, who is loving and who is fearful.

Conditioned by instincts and their sensory organs, dogs have their own view of the world. They are independent, highly sensitive beings. In our dogs' view of the world, we are at its center. It is us they recognize as their pack leaders. We determine the parameters of their lives. They are devoted to us, and in our company, they feel safe. If we are willing to accept their view of the world and show them affection, then they will return it a thousand times.

RELATIONSHIPS

We want our young dog to be capable and confident. It is the trainer's job to make sure that the dog has opportunities as a puppy to build up self-confidence and to develop endurance and willingness to take risks. The main person in a dog's life is the dog's main support system for building his self confidence. The dog will need his owner all of his life. Without his owner, the dog will never live up to his full potential.

The handler's temperament and attitude toward his young dog will affect the dog's devel-opment. Those who cannot show their dogs a lot of affection would do better not owning a dog. Otherwise there will be nothing but disappointment on one side and unhappiness on the other.

The more trustingly the young dog looks up to his owner and the more secure he feels in his care, the greater is the chance that the dog will become an ideal housemate and a valiant guard dog. A despotic handler will frequently produce a submissive dog; an unpredictable or inconsistent handler an insecure dog.

If we are able to understand our dog's view of the world and treat him with respect and affection, training will be easy and fun for both dog and trainer.

The handler's attitude toward the young dog will affect the pup's temperament as he grows and develops.

Setting the
RULES
✓ Sit
✓ Stay
✓ Heel
✓ Down

If the puppy decides to chew on the "forbidden" carpet, simply loosen his grip and carry him away by the nape of the neck.

A young dog will naturally act according to his drives and instincts. His head is filled with things that we consider mischievous. It is not his fault that his actions do not always meet with our approval. He does not know any better!

BEGINNING WITH DAY ONE

We must make it clear to the puppy at once what he is not allowed to do. This is foundation for later obedience training. An untrained dog will only cause us a lot of problems.

Let's keep in mind that our puppy should not be frightened or roughly intimidated by us. The temptation is great to reprimand him sharply when he does wrong, but we do not want a suspicious, insecure, or submissive companion, which could easily be the result of such behavior.

Fortunately, there are other ways. We warn the youngster when he is about to do something undesirable. This requires continuous supervision, but at this stage it is necessary anyway. It does not really matter whether we use a warning word or produce a threatening primal sound—the important thing is that we are ready.

The youngster will not yet understand our words. However, he will take his cue, with astonishing intuition, from the tone of our voice. What we have to do in this case is "growl," so to speak. If the young pup does not react to our warning, we give our warning more emphasis by increasing the volume without allowing it to become yelling.

In this natural non-violent way, the novice dog handler learns to directly convey his wishes to the dog. However, he must also be determined to follow through. The dog, with his incredibly sensitive intuition, will know immediately whether we are serious with our warning sound, whether the matter is not all that important to us, or whether we doubt our ability to get our way. Without being aware of it, we tell him by the tone of our voice.

The warning sound should always be the same and should be used by all members of the family. Whenever he is about to do something undesirable, he should immediately hear this sound. It is so important that this method is employed from the very first day and continued throughout the dog's life—both with puppies and adult newcomers.

THE CHEWING PHASE

The unavoidable eruption of teeth causes the pup to want to chew on all sorts of objects, but it is just a phase and will disappear when teething time is over. It is impossible for the puppy not to chew, but he can learn what not to chew. Of course, we must not let the pup out of our sight and we must be ready with our warning "growl." Sticking a "legal" chew object into his mouth prevents him from chewing on our shoes or furniture, and satisfies him at the same time.

We must provide the puppy with a variety of toys on which he can safely sharpen his teeth. Nylabone® makes a wide array of durable nylon bones and toys, as well as safe molded rawhide products and healthy edible treats. It's best to provide the pup with something new every now and then

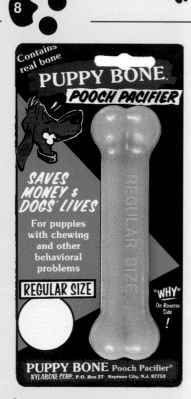

As your puppy's adult teeth grow in, he'll want to chew on anything to relieve the pressure. Better to offer a safe and solid chewing device than sacrifice your furniture. Give your pup a Puppybone® by Nylabone® and know that you're helping his teeth and gums to mature while he can chomp as hard as he likes. Available at your local pet shop.

to keep him interested—and to keep his mind off of your new shoes.

If it should happen that we don't catch him in time or that he, despite our warning, devotes himself to chewing on the carpet, then we calmly—but firmly—loosen his teeth, grab him by the nape of the neck, and carry him a short distance away. This demonstrates our dominance to him. In case of a repetition we may even shake him a little by the nape of the neck. This is a method that he can understand— canine parents pull at their kids quite a bit when they

disobey, but only then. There must be some discipline.

STEALING

Continuous supervision will also prevent the inclination to steal. Although most dogs are not members in the fellowship of thieves, it would be better to remove temptation. A dog, left to his own devices, may succumb to temptation if it should turn out to be a pleasurable experience.

BEGGING

Never are our canine friend's eyes as soulful as when he wants something: to go for a walk, to be petted, or to taste some delicacies from our dinner table. The latter is often not desirable or healthy, but it is difficult to resist those pleading eyes. What to do? We have two choices: either we allow our "partner" to share our breakfast and dinner (he will never forget to show up at the right time), or we say "no begging!" and consistently keep our meals to ourselves. If we soften even

once, we are lost. As hard as it may be, resist from the beginning.

LICKING

Licking is based on a primal instinct, especially with bitches. Puppies emit an aroma that causes the mother to clean them and stroke them with her tongue.

Also, according to their concept of hygiene, dogs want to heal their own or other dogs' minor injuries by licking them. If they love us, they will want to bestow their generosity upon us as well.

As long as it is no more than a little kiss as thanks for our petting him, it is acceptable, perhaps even an honor and a pleasure. However, when the desire to lick gets out of hand, it becomes a bother. How can we remedy this?

Since licking comes from a good natural instinct, we cannot attack it. We must ask ourselves why some dogs lick. It seems that the people dogs lick exude an aromatic stimu-

To combat boredom and relieve your dog's natural desire to chew, there's nothing better than a Roar-Hide™. Unlike common rawhide, this bone won't turn into a gooey mess when chewed on, your dog won't choke on small pieces of it, and your carpet won't be stained by it. The Roar-Hide™ is completely edible and is high in protein (over 86%) and low in fat (less than 1/3 of 1%). They come in different sizes, so there's one that will be just right for your dog. Available at your local pet shop.

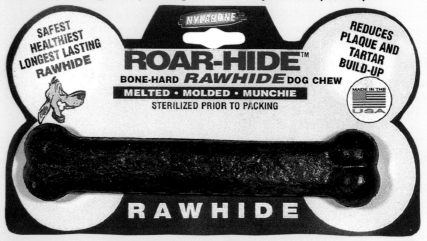

lus for the dogs' sensitive noses that, just as with the puppies, induces them to lick. If this is true it may be helpful to overlay this aroma with a harmless counterscent, such as lemon juice, scented soap, or perfume. Since body odors are individually different, we must test the "countermeasures" with the dog present. If he rejects the aroma by sneezing, we have found the solution.

JUMPING UP

This is an instinctive act that puppies perform with

way in which lively puppies work off their overflowing joy at seeing us. It is best just to not reward this behavior. Stand with your arms folded across your chest and your eyes diverted from the dog until he stops jumping on you. Ask him to sit. When he does so, then give him a happy greeting. Teach the pup to sit or stand when greeting people.

PROBLEMS IN YOUR ABSENCE

If the youngster commits a misdeed without having been warned in advance, he cannot

Only to be used as a last resort, the raised knee will stop your dog from jumping up.

an opportunity arises, he will use it. All we can do is think about how we may prevent this undesirable activity.

One solution for the digger would be to repair the hole and surround it with something to block off the area. A solution for the dog who likes to curl up on the bed when no one is home is to simply close the door.

Jumping up can be discouraged by bending down to the dog, thus removing the incentive for him to jump up.

Why would you want to give your dog a Carrot Bone™? Because you know carrots are rich in fiber, carbohydrates, and vitamin A. Because it's a durable chew containing no plastics or artificial ingredients of any kind. Because it can be served as-is, in bone hard form, or microwaved to a biscuit consistency—whichever your dog prefers. Because it's a 100%-natural plaque, obesity, and boredom fighter for your dog. Available at your local pet shop.

adult dogs. It mostly takes place in greeting and serves both as a way of establishing body contact and a demonstration of submissiveness. Fortunately, only a small number of young dogs are inclined to behave like this towards us. But they are quite capable of indulging in this pleasure until old age unless we take action.

At three months of age, this bad habit often starts. It is the

know that he is doing something that is forbidden. Let's assume he has, behind our back, dug his first big hole in the backyard. Even if we were to stake out the area and catch him in the act when he returns to indulge his newest passion, it would not help in the long run. The clever rascal has already learned that no warning will stop him if he goes to work when there is no one to see him. Thus, if such

If we want to stop independent journeying, only a sturdy fence will do. Punishing the dog on his return is senseless, even harmful. The dog's expectation of punishment would encourage longer and longer absences. Dogs do not associate their "escape" with the often customary punishment on their return. But they can associate their return with punishment, even if this is not what the owner had in mind.

If we prevent dogs from practicing bad habits in their youth, there is hope that they will not revert to these habits later, even if an opportunity to do so should present itself. That is the reason why it is so important to put a stop to any undesirable behavior at once.

Your puppy should never associate coming to you with fear or punishment. He should always come willingly and happily.

If he's not feeling well, your dog may act out, or will not respond wholeheartedly to training. Feeding him a proper diet, which contains pure lamb protein and wholesome grains, could give him the ingredients he needs for overall good health and responsiveness. Photo courtesy of Nature's Recipe Pet Foods.

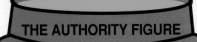

The Authority Figure

The goal of teaching a puppy what not to do is not limited to ridding the youngster of bad habits. Rather, the handler learns to give commands in an appropriate manner, and the dog learns to respond to them. This is also the best basis for obedience training.

The trainer himself must determine by trial and error what method is suitable for the individual dog. Teaching what is forbidden is the best way for a novice dog trainer to develop authority over his young student. Without question, authority must be established in this early phase of development because the pup's willingness to subordinate himself is still strong at this time.

The handler must learn to insist that his commands be obeyed, and he must be determined and not give up until the dog does as he is told. This is very important!

Experienced handlers usually possess enough authority to control a dog, but novices need some practice. A good way to practice being authoritative is by working with "prohibition" exercises. For instance, one could show the puppy a bone, but forbid him to take it immediately. The puppy will only get it after he has obeyed a command, such as "leave it." Of course, he will also receive lots of praise when he takes it on the command "take it." Such obedience exercises have a much more lasting effect if they are practiced in early youth. Later, it can be useful to occasionally refresh these lessons.

Usually, there are sufficient opportunities in everyday life to establish taboos and to exercise authority. Very self-confident dogs may attempt, now and then, to disregard a command, thus gently challenging our authority. Of course, under no circumstances may we give in, or else our friend will slowly but surely become too much for us to handle. This is the reason for establishing the necessary limits from the very beginning.

PUNISHMENT

Punishment does not build authority. At best it teaches

A bamboo stick or another object blocking the doorway tells the pup "Do Not Enter." We must enforce such rules at an early age so we do not have to resort to stricter measures later.

the dog to fear his unpredictable master, and thus become insecure. This is the exact opposite of what we want to accomplish.

It has been scientifically proven that any punishment that does not immediately follow the undesirable behavior is meaningless as a train-

ing measure because the dog does not understand the purpose of the action. Nevertheless, many dog owners swear that their dogs know exactly when they have done something wrong. "You should see how guilty he looks!"

These people are wrong! The behavior that they imagine is an expression of guilt is really an instinctive gesture of subordination. In the pack, lower-ranking dogs display this type of behavior in order to appease an angry superior. In most cases, this works just fine within a canine family. However, in the man-dog relationship, misunderstandings arise. The master's threatening posture alone is enough to make a dog assume a submissive position, even if he has a clear conscience. In time he may learn to make a connection between coming home and getting punished. However, to connect the act of running away with the punishment he receives upon his return is too complicated for a dog's brain.

If we are fortunate enough to catch the dog in an act of disobedience, then this is the occasion to teach him a lesson. It is most effective to grab the dog by the nape of the neck, lift him up (not with large breeds, of course), and shake him. This measure can only be recommended for extremely stubborn dogs or very serious misdemeanors. Another appropriate form of discipline is to place your grip over his muzzle. We grab the dog's muzzle from above and hold his mouth shut for a length of time appropriate for the misdemeanor committed. The dog will understand these types of punishment since they imitate canine behavior.

An owner must apply the rules of pack structure and understand the behaviors that dogs interpret as demonstrating submission or dominance in order to successfully train his dog.

Early Training

HOUSEBREAKING

Dogs, by nature, are very clean. Young puppies will make efforts not to soil their nest as soon as they are able to leave it. The larger their area of activity becomes, the further away they move from their bed in order to relieve themselves. It is up to the breeder not to allow these instincts to go to waste. Puppies can be housebroken in a few days as long as we are very attentive in our training; if not, it can take a lot longer.

⬆ **If your puppy shows any "suspicious" behavior, rush to get him outside as quickly as possible. Don't panic, though, as this will only frighten the pup.**

⬇ **Having the dog's bed next to the owner's bed will quickly alert the sleeping owner should the dog show signs of needing to go outside in the middle of the night.**

It is easiest for the pup to perform what we wish of him if he can do it as close as possible to his home and if his caregiver keeps him company. This will make him feel secure. It is a big advantage if there is a suitable grassy or sandy spot in the immediate vicinity of the house for the puppy to use. This simplifies the problem considerably because a young puppy has to go rather frequently.

Keeping an eye on the youngster proves to be advantageous. Whenever he gets restless, scoop him up and take him to the appointed place to relieve himself. It is important to always take the youngster to the same place—the familiar routine and the familiar scent will help him get into the habit of eliminating there. Of course, the pup will not announce that he has to go, so it is the job of his caregiver to watch for warning signs and to make sure that he is taken out regularly.

The pup will have to go out the first thing every morning and the last thing every night, after long rest periods, after meals (that should be served at the same time every day), and after play time, and whenever he creates "suspicion" by sniffing around restlessly.

During the first few days it is important that the same person always takes the pup outside. This person can watch for and learn the puppy's signals that he has to go out and develop a special sense of "danger" until the whole matter becomes routine. It won't take long until the youngster is capable of controlling his bodily functions and it won't be necessary to take him outside as often.

By the way—if an accident should happen on a carpet, it is imperative to treat the spot with a strong disinfectant to eliminate the odor and to prevent reoccurrence. You can find a good odor neutralizer in the pet shop.

THE DOG/OWNER BOND

Establishing a bond with our dog is a task we start from day one. A strong bond is the prerequisite for reliable obedience. The first days that a dog

A pup sees you, his owner, as a substitute parent; therefore, it is instinctive for him to follow you and try to stay as close to you as possible.

spends with his new owner build the foundation for their future relationship. Whether dog or owner has the upper hand is frequently decided in this short period of time. In order for a dog to be obedient, he must trust his owner, and this trust must first be developed.

In the wild, pups instinctively try not to lose contact with their parents. Otherwise their chances of survival decrease dramatically. This instinct serves for the preservation of the species and still exists in our domesticated dogs. This gives us, as our new pup's substitute parents,

a one-time opportunity to bond with him in an unforced way. By nature, this instinct is in effect for only a short time. Afterward, it must be replaced by force of habit.

This instinct to attach himself to us and to stay as close as possible to us is part of the young dog's make-up. All of the puppies that I have raised were, in the beginning, anxious to stay close to me. They ran after me on their own and kept a sharp watch out for me. There was no need to call them. At this stage, it is smart to start using whatever word you will be using for recall, so that the puppy learns to connect this word with his coming to you.

Call the puppy while walking away from him. This is a proven method to attract the youngster. If we pet him on the throat and forechest after he has come, he will be in heaven. This way he learns from the very beginning to attach himself to us and to stay with us, especially outside his home territory.

This is one of the foundations for the entire task of dog training: it should be consistently practiced from day one.

A puppy may be more inclined to come to you if you crouch down to make yourself appear smaller and closer to his level.

TAKE IT EASY!

It is all too common for the inexperienced dog owner to walk toward the puppy and grab him. After all, he would do the same thing with his own children. However, such behavior will have an intimidating, if not terrifying, effect on a young dog. The dog will often try to get away as quickly as possible whenever something moves rapidly toward him. This, in turn, will lead the "catcher" to attempt to catch the youngster by surprise, since he sees it as the only way to get a hold of him.

What will be the result? A nervous, insecure puppy that may become fearful and hand-shy. He will never have the courage to come to his handler.

COME FRONT

This exercise is somewhat more difficult for the puppy and only works if he trusts us completely. The pup sees us standing in front of him and facing him as an aggressive position. We can make it easier for him in the beginning by backing away from him or crouching down, perhaps while clapping our hands encouragingly.

We must reward the puppy with praise and petting when he comes as we want him to. He loves voice contact and being cuddled, and to him, our praise is reward enough for completing a task.

If the need arises to get a hold of the pup in a hurry, then positioning ourselves to one side of the dog will avoid the fear-inducing aggressive-looking frontal approach. If we crouch down low, most canine kids will come running without hesitation.

LEASH TRAINING

As soon as the puppy has reached the point that he follows us reliably, we can accustom him first to a light leather collar and then to a leash of normal length. Get him used to the collar and leash by letting him wear them around the house, and then practice walking him on the leash within the safe confines of your home or fenced yard.

The puppy should always be led on a loose leash; under no circumstances should we forcefully pull the youngster toward us with the leash. As soon as the puppy resists the leash, it is best just to drop it. In most cases he will soon come after us on his own if we move far enough away from him.

After we have reached the point that the pup always follows us on the lead around his immediate home territory, we can take him for a walk around the neighborhood.

The first critical moment comes when he is to leave his comfortable home and set out into the great unknown. If he is still too shy to do it on his own, carry him a few yards. If he immediately pulls toward home, then he is not yet ready for such an undertaking and we can try again another time.

Once we overcome this hurdle, the pup will stick to our heels very closely. This strange environment with its many new impressions makes him insecure, and under no circumstances would he want to lose us. The more independent and the more adventurous the dog is by nature, the sooner he will be ready to allow his own interests to divert him. This must be considered a positive development and we should permit him some liberties and let him sniff to his heart's content, since odors are so important to a dog. With a leash, we can reliably control the dog now, as a puppy, and later, when he is grown up.

The young dog will feel insecure away from his home environment and will follow his owner without any problem. A leash, however, is strongly recommended.

Learning Basic Commands

Making training interesting and fun will build up the pup's capability to learn and his joy of learning. As soon as the youngster has settled in—the latest at age three months—he is ready to learn something. If we go about it with skill and cleverness, he will enthusiastically participate.

WHY DOGS SHOULD LEARN

At about 10 weeks of age, a puppy is mature enough to start his training. At this stage of his development the ability

The choke collar must be put on so that the end with the ring to which the leash is attached runs across the top of the dog's neck.

and joy of learning awaken and his intelligence begins to develop. This has been proven through experience, and we should certainly take advantage of this information. The youngster's desire to establish a firm relationship with his "human being" is another favorable factor.

This is also an opportunity for inexperienced dog owners to gain experience in handling their dogs and to acquire the necessary authority. The earlier, the better.

Dogs are pack animals, and it is quite normal for them to subordinate themselves to a "pack leader" on whom they can rely and whose authority they recognize. A trusting, affectionate companion is a constant joy to his master. In this way, both man and dog profit from the training.

We should give the puppy two to three weeks to settle into his new home before he starts "school." For an adult newcomer, it is never too late to acquire certain rules of behavior. Until a dog is about eight years old, he will still be able to learn many things, even if not as easily as when he was still a puppy. Transplanted into a strange world, he, too, will strive for contact

with his new "family."

The usual obedience exercises, built into everyday life, facilitate communication between man and dog. They provide a means to direct the dog in the desired way.

Furthermore, doing things together means being able to communicate with one's dog. It is so comforting when our dog hears commands such as:

- "Stay!" and he stays behind, both at home and in the car.
- "Go out!" and he runs down the stairs ahead of us, or he knows that he may now run free.
- "Heel!" and he walks obediently on our left side at a critical situation on a walk.

Our dogs are capable of learning all this and more—the sooner, the better. The earlier he learns, the sooner we will be able to enjoy the benefits of a well-trained dog.

The prerequisite for happy cooperation between teacher and student is that we avoid any form of pressure or force. Pressure or force only intimidates our dog and makes him insecure. If we expect our dog to do something, we must entice him to do it. This calls for diplomacy, intuition, and skill. This is the basic difference from teaching him what *not* to do whenever we want to prevent undesirable actions. There, in accordance with our dog's temperament, we may occasionally even be somewhat rough—never, however, reacting in anger.

Thus, when in doubt, the trainer should ask himself the question: "Is the puppy supposed to do something or not to do something?" But how do we make clear to our dog what we want him to do?

We begin, of course, with the easiest lessons. At first, all practice should take place inside the house. Here our pupil is the most receptive to any form of learning because he is bored. Also, during early training it should always be the same person, if possible, who does the teaching.

When the puppy has learned a lesson, we continue practicing. Puppies will quickly get bored with long repetitive training sessions, so practice for a short time at frequent intervals. When the youngster's attention begins to wander, stop. Sometimes it is good to have a few "vacation days." Also when using treats for motivation, slowly decrease their use. He eventually must learn to work without treats, only with praise.

SIT

To teach the sit, we entice our pupil to come to us by holding up a treat. Then, when he stands expectantly in front of us, we hold the treat about eight inches above his nose. At the same time, move slowly towards him and say in a clear, calm voice, "Sit."

I have yet to meet a puppy that will not sit at this action.

You can entice your pup to sit by holding a treat about 8 inches above his nose while moving slowly toward him and saying "sit."

Hold the treat below the pup's mouth to offer it to him. This makes it easier for him to sit and wait for it obediently.

Holding the treat up too high will not keep the dog sitting; instead, he will jump up for it impatiently.

aggressive behavior, or other misdemeanors before they get started.

HEELING OFF LEAD

It is best to introduce the whole concept of heeling by working off lead first. Our dog will thus associate walking alongside us as a pleasant experience rather than a yanking, confusing experience. To begin, we lure the dog to our left side and hold a treat, hidden in our hanging left hand, in front of his nose. With the command "heel," we walk off. The youngster will gladly allow himself to be led in any direction by the hand holding the treat. If we lead him past some "guide surfaces" such as cabinets, walls, etc., he will learn at the same time to stay close at our side.

Whenever we come to a stop, the sit command is given and the youngster is given his reward whenever he successfully sits. It makes it easier for the dog to sit correctly if we move our left hand with the reward in a swinging arc to our left side. It is of some help in the beginning if we hold him back visually with the hand holding his reward whenever he does not immediately sit.

TURNS

The right turn is easy and almost automatic. When we perform an about face to the left our dog is expected to come after us, return to our left side, and sit. This works without effort if, at the moment of turning, we slip the reward into our right hand and move it behind us in front of the dog's nose, then place the treat back into our left hand and let the youngster

In order to keep his eyes on the treat, the pup must hold his head back, and, in so doing, naturally goes into the sit position. Walking backwards with his head held high is apparently uncomfortable, and thus the youngster chooses the path of least resistance and sits without being forced. We offer the sitting dog his reward from below his mouth. That makes it easier for him to wait obediently.

DOWN

In order to induce our young friend to lie down, we first make him sit and then we squat right next to him. We place our left hand lightly upon his lower back to prevent him from getting up. We place the right hand, holding a treat, on the ground in front of the sitting dog in such a way that he can just reach it if he were to lie down. But we will give him his reward only after he has laid down on the command "down."

This procedure does away with the usual pushing-to-the-ground-by-force method. Most puppies will catch on surprisingly quickly. Of course, it will take time until he will reliably sink to the ground whenever he hears the word "down." However, the effort is worthwhile because this exercise provides us with a marvelous tool to slow down our dog if he is not in immediate reach. A firm "down" can stop, for example, escaping, jumping up, undesirable have it when he obediently sits next to us as he has learned. Remember, such games are lots of fun for the puppy. Nevertheless, we always practice them only for a short time. At this age, the puppy's attention span is relatively short.

STAY

A very useful lesson is the sit-stay. Here we proceed first with our dog sitting in front of us.

We give him the command, speaking firmly and stretching the word "s-t-a-y," while simultaneously stepping slowly backwards—at first only a little bit.

As a reinforcement, we may stretch out one arm with the palm of the hand turned toward the youngster to create

Changing the dog's position from in front of the handler to the handler's left side—the right hand with the treat lures the dog past the right side to the rear.

The treat moves behind the handler's back from the right hand to the left, and the puppy follows it along.

When the treat stops moving, the "sit" command is given. The pup is given his reward when he sits successfully.

↑ **The sit-stay is taught in steps. With the dog sitting, move backwards slowly while giving the command "stay" and holding up your hand with the palm facing the dog.**

↑ **The "down" is easy to teach: Crouch down next to the sitting dog with one hand on his croup to prevent him from getting up and coax him down with a treat placed on the ground.**

a visual barrier. At the first sign that he may get up, we "growl." Getting up is not allowed! But whenever he obediently stays in the sit, we soon return to him and reward him.

Slowly we will increase the distance that we step back and later we may even disappear from his sight and wait a little longer before returning to him and giving him his reward. Don't forget the reward!

In the same way, we practice the down-stay. In the beginning we move backwards slowly while saying "stay" and raising a stopping hand.

HEEL ON LEASH

Not until the sit command is carried out reliably can we even think about teaching our puppy to heel on a leash. Almost all young dogs will pull with all their might whenever they are on a short lead. Pulling them back roughly is not always the best solution. It is better to come to a stop and command the dog to sit by means of a brief jerk on the

lead whenever he forges ahead. Then we continue on with the command "heel." If he begins to pull again, we start all over—even if at first it happens every three yards. In time, he will get sick of it and will learn to heel on leash without pulling.

SIT-HEEL

These two commands, used repeatedly in quick succession, are a good way to lead our friend peacefully past locations where he would love to make a scene. A watchdog on the other side of a gate or something suspicious approaching are quite capable of rattling the otherwise best-behaved dog.

Our actions, which demand a positive response from the dog, distract his attention from whatever excites him. If there are stimulating distractions such as fast-moving automobiles on a narrow road, motorcycles, children, or dogs running by, we should ask our dog to sit and distract his attention with a treat. This way, he will get used to the events that once overexcited him and will learn to meet them with composure.

RETRIEVING

This is a tricky task because it requires a whole series of actions, and demands a certain amount of discipline. It may be too difficult for a puppy to learn all at once, so it is better to start off with a few individual aspects of the task.

As a preliminary exercise, we take a small dog biscuit and roll it ahead of us as far as we can. Of course, the youngster will race after it immediately, search for it, and pick up a relatively large object and bring it to the handler. First, we encourage our dog to carry along his favorite toy. If he enjoys doing this, we stick the toy into his mouth during the obedience exercises. The next step is to induce the youngster to voluntarily surrender his toy. It is only natural that he would prefer keeping it for himself.

The "give" is best practiced separately. We make the dog sit in front of us, and we sit down ourselves. Then we place his toy into his mouth, let him hold it for a while, and then take it away again, rewarding the dog with a treat. It must be done in such a way that the youngster

You can practice retrieving by throwing an object, such as a small ball, and having the pup return to you with it.

eat it. Then he is recalled, returns to the handler, asked to sit in front of the handler, and then receives an additional morsel. He is asked to walk around the handler to his left side, and again is given a treat. After that, the whole process is repeated. The youngster learns it easily and has great fun doing it. Soon, the treat awarded for sitting in front can be eliminated.

Next, we will replace the thrown biscuit with a small object that will roll, but that is not suitable for either eating or playing with. The youngster should pick it up out of habit and return with it as usual. At this point, we should not be upset if he drops it on the way back. If the youngster runs after a thrown object and returns to the handler, that's already a small success.

The object of retrieving is that the dog is supposed to

A preliminary exercise for retrieving is to roll a treat across the floor and encourage the dog to "go get it."

START EARLY!

By the age of five to six months, all dogs should respond reliably to basic obedience commands. They should be comfortable and relaxed in their surroundings and they should behave in accordance with the wishes of their owners.

Where some serious dog sportsmen frequently approach training with deadly seriousness and thus tend to overdo it, many other dog fanciers believe that we should allow our puppies an unfettered youth. I used to belong to this group myself.

In the meantime, I have learned that we can give our puppies no greater joy than teaching them, in an unforced manner, all sort of things. They have a natural eagerness and desire to learn new things. Starting basic training in puppyhood is the only way to obtain a well-behaved dog at an early age.

The "give" is practiced separately. After retrieving the object, the dog should sit in front of his owner and let his owner take the object from his mouth.

cannot get away from us; starting out in the corner of a small room may be best.

It is important that the dog learns, on his own, that we will play an entertaining chasing game with him when he brings back the retrieved object. If we make no progress with this task then it is better, for the time being, to let things take their natural course. The "family dog" does not have to master proper retrieving. The disciplined obedience work with the dumbbell does not begin until much, much later.

Steer your dog away from problem situations by diverting his attention with something he'll enjoy—like working for a treat. A good choice is something that's not only tasty, but highly digestible and naturally preserved to protect against dietary sensitivities. Photo courtesy of Nature's Recipe Pet Foods.

Development of Drives & Instincts

PLAYING

Just like the youngsters of all animals, puppies are almost always in the mood for play. Playing is one of the necessities of life. Fortunately, puppies are quite capable of entertaining themselves. To watch them play is pure joy. They are just like kittens and entertain themselves in a very similar manner. A large amount of time is spent with chewing games. Gnawing and tearing things are major urges.

All kinds of games of catch and grab are favorite pastimes and you can bet that anything that can be pushed around—like a ball or a stick—will be.

Lots and lots of toys are needed. They will direct the compulsory need to chew toward "legal" items. Play satisfies the puppy's urge for activity and develops intelligence and dexterity.

By arousing the dog's curiosity with an interesting object, you're inviting him to play.

Games that produce the greatest din provide the greatest enjoyment. Human participants are, of course, most welcome in these games. It's best to crouch down to the puppy's level. Playing along is not difficult and no limits are set for our inventiveness.

During this early period, there is absolutely no need for these games to be learning-oriented. All we care about is that the youngster have fun and that we are in close contact with our four-legged housemate.

CHASE GAMES

These types of games are both popular and instructive. The human player runs away holding a swinging bag or rag.

Most canine kids will be enthusiastic participants wanting to pursue and grab the phantom prey. There then ensues a merry game of tug-of-war. When the youngster has got a really good hold of the bag, we hold a treat in front of his nose and say "out." In most cases, he will decide in favor of the bait, especially if the whole game will then start anew.

Many dogs think it great fun to search for thrown objects in high grass, leaves, or similar localities. Potatoes are especially well suited for this. At first we throw them a short distance, later a greater distance. This is where the pup's hunting instinct will come out.

PROTECTION GAMES

The instinct to defend property is probably the most desirable characteristic of the valiant family dog. After all, as an adult, he will be expected to protect his owner's home and property against infringements. This instinct must be inherited.

A puppy does not yet have enough "personality" to protect the home, but he is quite capable of protecting his bone.

Thus, we present out youngster with a delicious juicy bone or a chew toy that he will immediately make his own. His owner will stand or

To maximize the effects of training, your dog needs to be healthy and alert—the products of a good diet. One that combines vegetables and high-quality meats for maximum nutrition and palatability. Photo courtesy of Nature's Recipe Pet Foods.

sit next to him as another familiar person pretends to want to take away the bone. As soon as the dog begins to growl he has won the game!

It must not be the goal of our training to tease him to such a degree that he loses his cool—which would not be difficult. This would only make him insecure and perhaps even unpredictable. On the contrary, he is to learn that his growling will be respected. Dogs do that, of course, to each other as well. That is part of the species' code of etiquette. Never did I observe a dog taking something away from another dog, even if he was the smallest and weakest, if he defended it with a determined growl.

The more calmly a dog growls, the more secure he feels. The more precarious he thinks his situation, the wilder his response. This depends, in part, on the given situation. If he attacks, then that is a last desperate attempt to snatch victory from

the jaws of defeat. Many dog fanciers see this quite differently. That is why we do not let things get this far when teaching protection. Under no circumstances must we conduct these experiments with the regular meals. That may lead to disagreeable incidents in the future.

I was once bitten hard in the leg without warning by a

visiting dog who was otherwise thoroughly gracious. Unsuspectingly, I had come too close to him while he was eating his meal. Later, his owners admitted that they had repeatedly provoked him during meal time, to the point that he attacked, in order to make him more aggressive. This was the cause for this unpleasant incident. Under normal circumstances, this dog would have growled first and I would have been warned.

Dogs that do not growl at all lack either the instinct to protect or the necessary confidence. Either may develop with time. We just have to test them occasionally.

ROUGHHOUSING

Mock fights with humans are also part of the training program. At first, the trainer will attempt to provoke the puppy to playful resistance by pulling on his tail. The puppy will grab with his whole mouth his human playmate's lower arm. We reply to this with quick grabs of the dog's ruff.

This future tracker keeps his eyes on a slowly disappearing tasty treat.

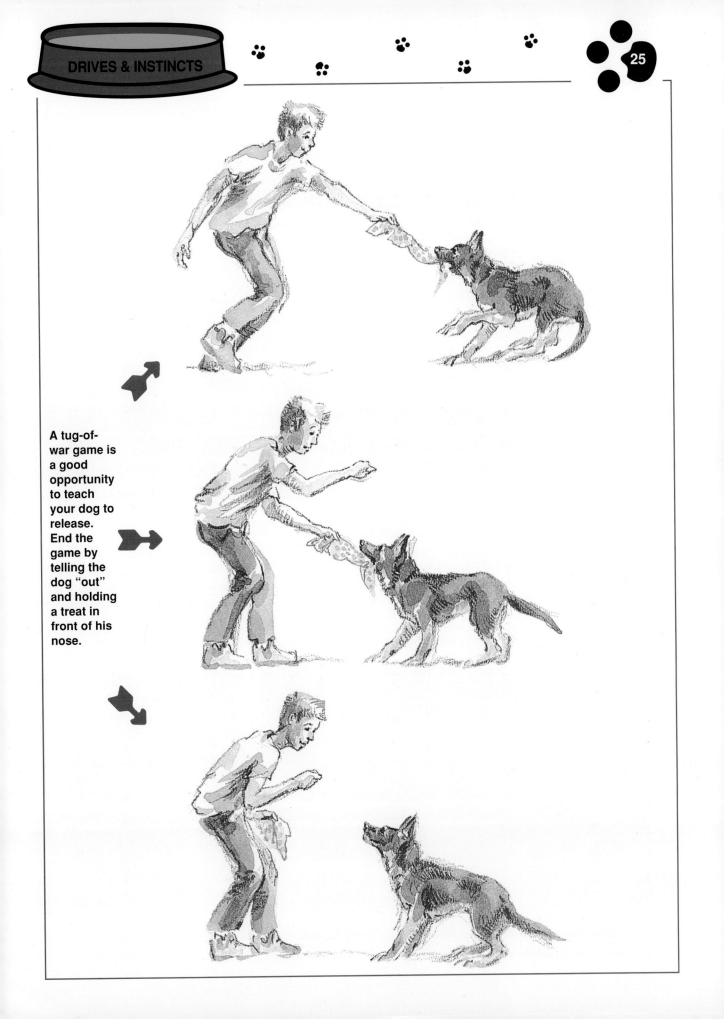

A tug-of-war game is a good opportunity to teach your dog to release. End the game by telling the dog "out" and holding a treat in front of his nose.

Children are always welcome as playmates.

Isn't roughhousing fun?

Should the youngster, in his eagerness, take too strong a hold, it is quite permissible to yelp and growl. Perhaps he still needs to learn how far he may go. After all, dog fur is far less sensitive than human skin. Those little teeth are still as sharp as needles. After

responding with a yelp and/or a growl, immediately end the "game." This teaches our puppy that serious rough-housing is a no-no.

Many youngsters are enthusiastic participants and others need to overcome some inhibitions. However, we must not play these

games to excess, especially not if our dog has an innate desire for them. They should not become a passion for the dog, other-wise we may have a fighter on our hands. It is always the human participant who terminates the game with an energetic "out!"

You *and* your dog will be contributing to the training program, so both of you should be eating right. A food that combines easy-to-digest wholesome grains and real venison meal may be best for dogs with dietary sensitivities to other meats. Photo courtesy of Nature's Recipe Pet Foods.

ADOLESCENCE

Don't underestimate a young dog. Here, a youngster stands his ground and protects his find against three adults.

This phase in the development of our dogs corresponds approximately to the rebellious age of our own teenagers. It brings new problems for us as dog owners.

Now, there are good, obedient dogs that present little problem, and there are those that look for adventure. Basically, the latter is a positive sign since it indicates a desired willingness to take risks. Nevertheless, we must put strict limits on this lust for adventure. Our dog's search for independence does not impair, however, his basic bond to his master. The "child" is turning into a "teenager" and, later, will become the companion we all hope for.

It may happen that our authority is challenged during doggy adolescence. Our clever friend may experience desires that put him into conflict with his accustomed obedience.

At this time, the prohibition training must be refreshed and augmented with educational games that practice obedience. What used to be friendly invitations to such activities now become more or less strict commands if our dog should not obey.

A CRITICAL PHASE

At about six months of age, all puppies go through a phase of noticeably altered behavior. They become visibly more "cautious" in their demeanor, which expresses itself in different ways, according to the pups' individual temperaments. Some are visibly more insecure, others become almost shy.

Presumably, this is an instinct that goes back to the time when dogs were still wild. It is probable that the parents' attention to caring for their young decreased at this age. The puppies had trustingly

Roughhousing can be a lot of fun for both the pup and his human playmate. Remember, though, that puppy teeth are needle-sharp—the pup should always be discouraged from biting.

relied on their parents' care up to that point, but as they got older, they had to start watching out for themselves. This, of course, would initially make them less secure.

The trainer should know this and should help his puppy regain his confidence. During this age period (approximately nine to eighteen months, though it varies between individuals and breeds), changes in environment and other potentially frightening experiences should be avoided as much as possible. The dog will find them much more difficult to deal with now than at other times. Our dogs may surprise us with their belligerence or naughtiness during adolescence, but remember, like teenaged children, it passes. Hang in there!

THE RUNAWAY

In this phase, many young dogs burst with energy and enterprise. Fortunately, the "runaway" phase does not last long. Working off energy through daily exercise and

Some puppies seem to have an endless supply of energy. They are interested in everything and will bound from one thing to the next.

You can help your dog work off excess energy by making sure that he gets regular exercise and activity. Exercising with your dog is beneficial for you, too.

activity may be helpful.

Sometime, for certain, our young friend will happen to take off in pursuit of a rabbit, a cat, or something of a similar nature. There is no need to immediately panic. The chances that he will cause trouble or lose his way are slim. The further he moves away from us, the more his desire for adventure wanes. Soon he will come racing back.

It would be unwise to welcome his return with a reprimand. Rather, we should hide somewhere in the vicinity. This represents a good opportunity to observe how our puppy will react in such situations. Some young dogs will begin immediately looking for their master's trail and, naturally, will discover him quickly. Others will become nervous and run about aimlessly. It is helpful to know what our dog's reaction will be.

This basket full of Shar-pei puppies may look innocent enough, but watch out! Naturally inquisitive puppies love to explore—set rules early and always supervise.

In the future, we should be on guard and not take our eyes off the youngster. No matter how much your dog wants to dash around to release energy, unless you're in an enclosed area, keep him on a collar and leash. Instead of examining the horizon for things that may arouse our dog's curiosity, we would do better to watch our rascal so that we may slow him down should the need arise.

Young puppies learn just how much they can get away with by roughhousing and play fighting with their littermates. Some pups always come out on top!

If our dog takes off in a large, enclosed area, we may be concerned about what mischief he may get into out of our reach. In such situations, the command "down," spoken in a sharp voice, has, at first, the effect of a brake on our dog. Sure, he is trained to lie down, but the exciting events around him get in the way of the correct execution of the command. How do we make the best of this situation?

Whenever I interrupt my dog Troll's intention to chase after something sensational, he will at first stand still. To lie down under such circumstances is absolutely beyond him. So I follow up immediately with the command "stand...stay," and I keep repeating this command, with an undertone of threat, until I can put the leash on him. Uninterrupted command contact is important. In this way we have come to an arrangement without losing our authority.

However, if our escapee is already at full speed and beyond our immediate area of control, then there is nothing we can do. There is no point in yelling after him! At full speed and with his ears laid back, he quite possibly cannot hear us. All we would achieve is drawing the attention and ridicule of others. Only after some time has passed can calling or whistling have any success.

A shrill whistle blast is most alarming when the dog is in a tense mood. For that reason, it is advisable to reserve the whistle blast for "special occasions" and not to practice it in training. Getting used to it would diminish its

effect. Those who cannot whistle with their fingers should put an "inaudible" dog whistle around their necks. It has the added advantage that human ears cannot perceive it and our misfortune is not made public.

Even when our escapee's goal is another dog, it would be pointless to yell after him - which, of course, we are inclined to do. We have no chance at slowing down the heedless youngster and will only unnecessarily upset the

You can recall your four-legged friend by using a dog whistle. Specially made whistles are inaudible to human ears.

other dog. It is better to keep our composure and signal to the other handler that our dog is friendly. Many dog fights come about only because of the fearful behavior of their owners.

Where is my master? I know he's here somewhere!

THE DOGGONE URGE TO CHASE

Of course, dogs that have inherited a strong urge to chase will tend to give in to these temptations. The young chaser hardly has any prospects for a successful hunt; he just enjoys the chase for the sake of the chase. It is difficult to specifically break him of this type of habit. If he is a compulsive chaser, you might try tying something to his collar that will get in the way of his legs when he starts galloping.

A strong chase instinct may, however, be dangerous if it induces the dog to chase cars and motorcycles. This can be prevented with, for example, a prong collar and a 10-foot lead.

One big happy (and well-behaved) family! Training and caring for multiple dogs takes a lot of time, commitment, and patience, but the loyalty and affection you get in return will be well worth your efforts.

Pulling is a bad habit that can be curbed by walking your dog in a special halter. Some halters are available in styles that can be used with dogs of any size. Photo courtesy of Four Paws.

Four Paws®
NO-PULL HALTER®

Medium
Black
Adjustable
fits necks
12"-17"

FOR MAXIMUM CONTROL WITHOUT CHOKING YOUR DOG

STOPS ANY DOG FROM PULLING

The No-Pull Halter is the only product guaranteed to stop any size dog from pulling while offering total comfort and safety for your dog.

Item #59500

 If used properly, the choke chain can be an effective training aid.

THE LEASH

The customary short leash severely limits a dog's mobility, especially if the handler also insists on perfect heeling. Dogs seem to find highly interesting information along the side of the roads. Should we really deprive them of this joy? If we cannot risk allowing our all-too-adventuresome friend to run free, there is one more solution: the long leash. There are leather leashes that are about a quarter-inch wide and eight to ten feet long, with a light-weight snap hook on one end. There are also light-weight leashes made out of nylon that are much cheaper. They have the advantage that they cannot be chewed up, but they can be too light for a number of purposes, and more difficult to hold on to.

If the need arises, the Flexi-lead can be shortened to keep the dog close at the handler's side.

Standing near a road with an even traffic flow, we hold the lead loosely. When the dog shows signs of starting to chase after a vehicle, we sharply give the command "down," immediately followed by "sit-stay" or "stand-stay." If the dog does not respond to the commands and takes off, he is jerked back sharply and thus introduced to the un-pleasantness of the prong collar. Although it sounds like rough treatment, remember that we are trying to override an instinctive action, one that could prove to be very danger-ous for the dog.

Along with the chase in-stinct comes the urge to run and romp. That is why we should incorporate a daily exercise program that in-cludes some running. This way we keep the desire to run under control and lessen the desire to escape.

A long leash grants our canine student at least limited freedom, but we still have reliable and stress-free control over him should a critical situation arise. We direct our trainee through the usual commands. The leash is just a safety rope.

However, working such a leash takes some getting used to. It will present no problem if, in the beginning, we use both hands. The leash should be loosely held without dragging on the ground. The best way to accomplish this is to hold the end of the leash in our right hand and to use the left hand to adjust for the varying distances. After a little bit of practice we will be able to manage with one hand.

This type of leash is long enough that our dog does not need to pull in order to pursue his favorite activity—intently sniffing everything. A short leash does not allow him to do this.

A Flexi-lead that can be set to desired lengths is another useful device. It can easily be kept short or it can be lengthened to allow limited freedom up to a radius of approximately 17 feet.

◄ Active breeds like the Border Collie will benefit from having the freedom to explore that a long leash offers.

▲ There are many different types of leashes available. The nylon leash has some advantages in that it is lightweight and the dog can't chew it up.

▼ The Flexi-lead can easily be kept short, or it can be lengthened to allow limited freedom up to a radius of approximately 17 feet.

The Dog's Social Behavior

A puppy interacts with his dam and littermates right from day one as he begins his education about life in a family "pack."

A dog must interact with all types of dogs—different breeds, different sizes—in order to develop good social behavior.

INTERACTING WITH OTHER DOGS

All puppies need to interact in early puppyhood with as many different dogs as possible if we expect them to later communicate without problems and not to become troublemakers. Social behavior is probably innate. Dogs, however, must practice their social skills in order to build up confident manners through experience.

Our puppy behaves differently every time he meets an unfamiliar dog. The various types of dogs he meets affect him in different ways. There

 Dogs often "challenge" each other, without the intent of inflicting pain, to see who will back down first.

Dogs need to be socialized with a variety of people as well as with other dogs. This German Shepherd Dog sniffs a stranger's hand as a way of "checking him out."

are large dogs and small dogs, wild dogs and gentle dogs, outgoing dogs and shy dogs, dogs he knows and dogs he doesn't know, etc. The temperament of the other dog affects our youngster's behavior in various ways. It appears that he will trust a calm and confident dog, but insecure types will trigger reservations in him.

It is important in such encounters that the dogs are at least on a loose lead. It is

very useful, especially for inexperienced dog owners, to observe how their young dog communicates with other dogs. Frequently we must help him overcome inhibitions, and experience is the best guarantee for success.

ACCEPTANCE INTO THE DOG FAMILY

What may happen during such encounters was shown to us by young Zola who came into our house at age 12 weeks. She came with us totally relaxed and spent the

Please—don't bite too hard!

Taking her puppy's muzzle into her mouth is a teaching measure that a mother dog uses on her young.

trip to our house on my lap. Immediately after we arrived, she began nonchalantly exploring her new home. The greeting she offered to our "big ones" was very tempestuous. She jumped wildly at Dally and Filou in attempts to lick their muzzles. I found that rather impertinent and had no idea that I was observing a puppy's desire to "calm the waters" with her superiors. In Zola's case, her attempts were somewhat hectic because she was a bit insecure.

Our males behaved with tolerance; however, if the puppy is too pushy, it may happen that his behavior becomes too much for the other dogs to handle. The youngster may have a furious growl directed at him as an indication of displeasure. This is a natural training measure in which we should not intervene. The youngster must learn that there are limits. This is for his own good. He will immediately demonstrate submissive behavior and thus appease the anger that he brought upon himself.

At the first encounter, the youngster is still very shy. He feels that the safest place is close to his owner, between her feet.

His courage grows as he becomes more interested in the other dog.

Progress is being made as the young dog moves a little farther away from his owner.

Because there is so much submissive devotion on the puppy's part, no adult dog would hurt a puppy.

PUPPY'S EMOTIONS

Should our canine kid, upon encountering another dog, become aggressive and rush at the strange dog with furious barking, this is no cause for alarm. He has no intentions whatsoever of attacking. Rather, our young hero finds himself in a conflict. On the one hand, he would love to establish a relationship with the other dog, but, on the other hand, he lacks the courage to do so. This form of aggressive behavior is a sign of insecurity and indicates that he does not feel quite up to the situation.

Dogs that rush at something while barking furiously generally have no intentions of attacking. They will stop in time. All they want to do is intimidate the other dog. That is the sole purpose of the exercise. Their handlers must know this in order to behave rationally and calmly.

Dog owners need to recognize their dogs' behavior to distinguish between whether they are just playing or actually displaying aggressive behavior.

It is mostly those youngsters whose nerves are a bit shaky who are inclined to such behavior. In any case, it would be senseless to encourage such behavior in the mistaken belief that this will produce a courageous dog. On the contrary, it is more likely that he will become unpredictable. It would be just as wrong to attempt to put a stop to this behavior through intimidating maneuvers. That way we would rob the youngster of the courage that he does have.

Early interaction with littermates helps to build a pup's confidence.

Instead, we strengthen his backbone by staying close to him and talking to him calmly with an exaggeratedly low voice. This way he is most likely to quiet down and become, in time, more and more confident and less nervous. We must weather this developmental phase with persistence.

INTERACTING WITH OTHER PEOPLE

Normally, our dogs live less in a canine world than in a human one. We must introduce them into the human world with great care from early puppyhood on.

So that our young friend does not become fixated exclusively on the main person(s) in his life, we should try to introduce him to as many different people as possible. It will make owning a dog considerably easier if we can entrust him occasionally to the care of other people without having to worry.

We should not be upset during this period if our puppy makes friends with anyone who plays with him. This is the way of puppies! However, we will also notice that he behaves quite differently toward people who do not like dogs. Dogs respond to the emotional state of the people they come in contact with.

Adult dogs feel instinctively whether they are dealing with well-meaning or unfriendly people, with harmless or suspicious ones, and behave accordingly. Their intuition will prove much more sensitive than ours. There is no reason to worry that our youngster might become too trusting.

It's meal time! A litter of four-week-old Australian Cattle Dog pups gathers around the food bowl.

"One at a time...don't push!" The benefits of dog ownership—unconditional love and loyalty.

 This German Shepherd Dog meets a new friend for the first time.

The greeting ritual of each dog sniffing the other's rear end will occasionally send the dogs around in circles.

A major goal of dog training should be to teach the dog good manners and good social behavior, and to be accepting of all friendly people.

Aggressive Behavior

BETWEEN DOGS

There is no need to worry when allowing juveniles to interact with other juveniles. Usually they will be well-behaved if trained from puppyhood. These contacts are very important. The dog is testing forms of social behavior and should meet as many breeds of dog as possible. In this way he will learn that all other breeds are dogs, too. Most walks will offer opportunities for such encounters, as will attending a puppy kindergarten. Your veterinarian can probably refer you to a trainer who conducts such classes.

The wildly bared teeth may look intimidating, but these dogs are engaged in nothing more than a harmless mock fight.

"This ought to get your attention!" Puppies often nip at each other in play, but they also let each other know when they are playing too rough.

42

On occasions when dogs are meeting, the owner of the young dog can see with his own eyes how harmless the encounters between well-adjusted dogs really are and how reasonably (hopefully) his own pup behaves.

However, we should avoid contact with openly fearful dog owners. They usually won't take any advice and their dogs, who are equally insecure, easily get embroiled in arguments.

JUVENILES AND ADULTS

No adult dog will seriously fight with a juvenile. However, it may happen that an adult will rudely rebuff a juvenile when the youngster's protestations of subordination become too much for him. After all, this is his right. This will be entirely sufficient to intimidate the youngster, and that is the purpose of the exercise. As long as we allow matters to take their course and do not unnecessarily interfere, there will be no danger.

Play time is more fun with a friend! These young Westie littermates share a toy.

Dogs need contact with other dogs. Supervised interaction between dogs should begin in puppyhood and continue throughout their lives.

Among dogs that know each other, it may happen that the older one feels the "need" to put down the juvenile who is near adulthood. Presumably, he wants to make clear that he is still the stronger one. However, a dog that is sure of his dominance does not need to do this.

WHEN DOGS MEET

There are many dog fanciers who strive to avoid any encounters between their four-legged friends and other dogs in the belief that all such encounters have to result in turmoil. Others are of the opinion that a well-brought-up dog should not have any interest in other dogs.

Thus, it comes about that many dog owners have no idea how their canine friends communicate with their own kind. They expect murder and mayhem, and behave accordingly. In reality, most accidental canine encounters are conducted in absolute peace because, under normal circumstances, there is no reason for fighting a weaker dog.

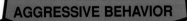

Adult dogs and puppies will not get into serious fights with each other, but it is often the adult's duty to put the youngster in his place.

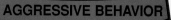
SURPRISE!

Whenever two dogs find themselves in a questionable situation, we should avoid doing anything that might shake their composure. All people involved should be as quiet as church mice. If we act at all, we should act only to calm matters down. If the situation threatens to become dangerous, a threat uttered in a low voice may be effective.

The best thing for the handlers to do is move away from the dogs in opposite directions. Taking away the moral support that the handlers' presence provides considerably diminishes aggression. Handlers are hesitant, however, to do so since they do not wish to create the appearance that they are evading responsibility. Nevertheless, in many circumstances, this is the only correct thing to do.

It is only the well-intentioned, but wrong, interventions of the dogs' owners that trigger many conflicts between dogs or intensify such confrontations and cause them to become out of control.

PROTECTED BY INSTINCTS

Matters can become dangerous when a large dog meets a little dog and the handlers lose their composure. After all, it is only natural to want to save the weaker dog.

A typical example of such an encounter: Recently, a close acquaintance told me, full of indignation, that her little Dachshund had been so badly bitten by a German Shepherd that she had to take him to the veterinarian. What interested me, of course, was exactly how this happened.

A free-running, curious

Large breeds often cause some people to panic or act fearfully and, unfortunately, these types of reactions can often cause a dog to react aggressively. ➤

German Shepherd approached her Dachshund, who immediately threw himself on his back. The bigger dog nudged the little dog's belly with his nose. The Dachshund's owner screamed in terror and the other owner jerked back his German Shepherd.

In reality, and in all probability, the dog had intended to do nothing worse than sniff the dog's belly. My acquaintance had misunderstood and, through her screaming, caused the handler of the larger dog to intervene. Startled, the Shepherd nipped, but definitely not bit, the little one's belly. Indeed,

A dog can gather a lot of information by using his keen sense of smell. It is said that dogs spend half their lives sniffing!

all that occurred was a slight scratch. The owner was honest enough to admit that she could have saved herself the visit to the veterinarian.

EXCEPTIONS PROVE THE RULE

Despite all this, occasionally canine encounters become brawls without the unreasonable behavior of the handlers being the underlying cause.

There are dogs that are quarrelsome by their very nature—a more frequent occurrence in some breeds than in others. Caution is advisable with very hyper or very nervous dogs that can easily lose their composure and may react unpredictably. Things become especially dangerous if this type of

These adult Boxers are very tolerant of their curious youngsters, but they will also let the pups know when enough is enough.

temperament is combined with the otherwise desirable instinct to protect. Such a dog is unsuitable as a family dog but is frequently valued as a guard or protection dog because of his aggressiveness and alert intelligence.

This type of nasty defensive reaction is typical of a younger, weaker dog.

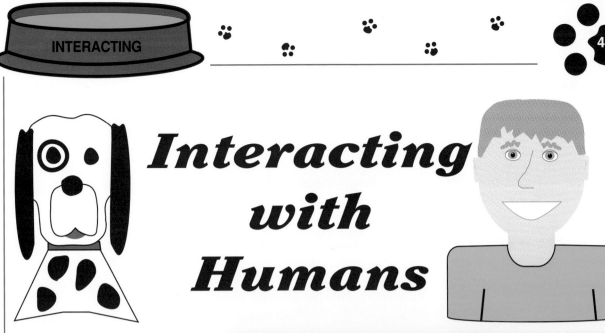

Interacting with Humans

There cannot be any question that a normal dog is equipped with a healthy inhibition against seriously hurting a human being. Normally, he will always attempt to achieve his goal (e.g., to protect his territory) through intimidation or threats. In most cases, he probably will be successful. Who would tangle without cause with a dog ready to fight? It is surely not desirable to remove this useful inhibition from family dogs.

In the majority of cases we will be facing a lot of trouble if our dog bites someone. Even the invading burglar can put on his most innocent face and deny all evil intentions and we are left with the blame. In our own home it is quite sufficient if the dog holds the intruder in place or announces him by barking. The important thing is that he does not let him in.

In an emergency when rage or fear—or both simultaneously—rule a dog's behavior, the bite inhibition may be overridden. This can, above all, be brought about by influences from the environment. We must not encourage this type of behavior in our training.

After you are comfortable with basic obedience, you can teach your dog more advanced commands. This Golden Retriever takes his favorite toy—his Gumabone® Frisbee®—over the high jump.
*The trademark Frisbee is used under license from Mattel, Inc., CA, USA.

THE MAIL PERSON

For some reason, many dogs dislike the mail delivery people. Dog and mailman jokes have become cliché. If the letter carrier does his duty and fills our mailbox, the dog will bark like crazy and would attack if he could. This animosity even extends to the postal vehicle, which many dogs can recognize from afar.

intentions at all.

Of course, these are entirely different emotions that may occur at the same time. Thus, we have the threatening barking where barking and growling alternate. He would like to protect but, deep down, does not feel strong enough. The more he growls, the stronger is his urge to defend. Nevertheless, such a perfor-

dealing with an intruder in our home or another threatening person, becoming excited ourselves will irritate the dog and increase his excitement. However, usually the presence of a large dog as companion or in the house is enough to deter crooks in the first place.

A dog's behavior in these situations, however, is determined not only by his tem-

Dogs can be quite protective of their territory, including their toys. This special toy, a Gumabone® Frisbee®, has a bone shape on top that makes it easy for dogs to pick up.

We should note that a dog who intends to defend something in earnest will behave in a calm manner and will signal his intentions with a threatening posture, possibly reinforced with growling. On the other hand, if he barks at the top of his lungs, he is just getting excited; the less secure he feels, the more excited he gets. He has no aggressive

mance is very impressive. After all, that is precisely the idea. If the opponent loses his nerve, the dog gets the upper hand.

If the dog becomes excited and starts displaying protective behavior toward harmless people, we should ask the people just to remain quiet and the dog will keep his distance. If we are indeed

perament but also by the circumstances in which they occur. A dog will be the most deliberate in the presence of his owner. Left to himself, he will be clearly less confident. He is more confident during daylight hours than at dusk or in the dark. He is more likely to stand his ground in the immediate vicinity of his home than far from home or

Tug-of-war can be fun for you and your dog, as long as you can safely end the game with the command "out" or a similar word that tells the dog to release the item.

To complete a retrieve, the dog returns to the handler with the item, sits in front of the handler, and allows the handler to take the item.

"Come on! I'm ready to play!" The more time that an owner spends with his or her dog, the stronger the bond that is formed.

on unfamiliar territory. He will be more relaxed after he has eaten than when hungry, etc.

We have to take all of these factors into account when we evaluate our dog's behavior. Furthermore, the behavior and the mood of the handler and of the other people involved contribute to how the events unfold.

The reason for the dog's animosity toward the mail person is that the letter carrier comes up to the house—the dog's territory—rattles at the mailbox, and then "cowardly" trots away again. Our dutiful dog considers this to be a hostile act that ignites his honest urge to defend his territory.

Thus, beware! Keep the dog away from the letter carrier and other messengers! Since it is no secret that letter

 You never know what your puppy will get his paws on or his teeth into!

 In order to behave by the rules, a dog must know the rules. What's to stop a dog from sticking his snooping snout into the garbage if he doesn't know any better?

carriers are welcomed in such an impolite manner by dogs, many post offices have established rules for their carriers regarding their behavior in the presence of dogs.

THE BITER

There are rowdy dogs even among breeds that are generally known as peaceable. Their stimulus threshold is so low that their innate aggression breaks through quickly. These types of dog are especially dangerous when they are suddenly released from enforced rest, e.g., from a kennel. Their tensions explode and they may charge at the closest victim. If, on top of that, they are received with screaming and/or defensive actions, their excitement increases.

If attacked in such a manner, try to stand still and perhaps talk calmly in a low voice. With trained dogs, the command "down" may help.

Biters do not belong in homes as housemates. They should serve somewhere else under the supervision of experts.

Something about being on a short leash triggers aggressive behavior—as the leash gets shorter, the dog becomes more aggressive.

A dog must be able to perform reliably on lead for advanced obedience work. This is Thornfield's Mister Mario, CD, and his owner Eileen Robinson.

AGGRESSION ON THE SHORT LEASH

The behavior of dogs on the short leash has a separate set of laws. Once, when I brought my five-month-old bitch Zola to the training site, she was greeted by a slightly older, unfamiliar bitch on a leash who was barking hysterically. Since Zola, running free, seemed totally unimpressed by this spectacle, I persuaded the owner of the bitch to let her dog off the leash. She resisted for a while, but finally gave in. Convinced that we were in for a fight, she was immensely surprised when her dog immediately sought refuge behind her. Then the

Training classes give owners the opportunity to expose their dogs to other dogs in a controlled setting.

bitch was willing, even if a bit hesitatingly at first, to establish cautious sniffing contact with Zola.

When Zola and I returned to the training site a week later, I had Zola on the leash. This time, she, too, broke into wild raving the moment she saw the other bitch, who again barked aggressively. All of this happened in spite of the fact that Zola had an absolutely steady temperament and had proven to be friendly and reliable when interacting with other dogs. Anyone who saw this spectacle would probably believe that these two bitches had nothing else in mind but to fight to the death.

Nevertheless, we risked letting both dogs off lead at the same time about ten yards apart. Both abruptly fell silent, leapt towards each other, sniffed each other in a tense posture, and started to

An advantage of using a longer lead is that the handler can control the amount of freedom that the dog is given.

play happily. All of this after such displays of aggression on the leash!

Perhaps we should ask ourselves why dogs behave in such a way. Suddenly, dogs with very good temperaments will behave like wimps. The inexperienced handler must think his dog a nasty fellow, but when the leashes drop it is revealed what his state of mind really is. But who would risk it?

We have tested such situations again and again and with a variety of dogs. However, we must take care that they are far enough apart when we set them free that, if need be, a shaky candidate can run away. Otherwise he might start a desperate fear attack, not a favorable situation.

Our dog Troll behaves in an absolutely self-possessed and superior manner around other dogs. However, whenever reasons of etiquette require that I hold him on a short leash, he is like a different dog. If a barking dog is led past us on a leash, I have to put Troll firmly under discipline—"Sit! Heel!, Sit! Heel!" and so on if I want to prevent him from behaving badly as well. Why that is, I'm not quite sure. Evidently, the very short leash somehow triggers aggression in dogs.

BEHIND FENCES

Behind fences, kennel gates, and car windows, we frequently observe wildly bared teeth and wrinkled noses and we pray that the

barrier may hold. Here, too, the obstruction causes the dogs to behave in a fashion that they would not display if they were unrestrained. We can say that the greater the fuss with which the "hero" threatens in order to intimidate, the more he is in need of it! After all, the spectacle has quite an intimidating effect, and this effect is most likely the point of the exercise.

One day, our Farna had a barking duel with the neighbor's dog. A hedge separated the two. Suddenly they came face to face with each other where there was a hole in the hedge. Immediately, Farna's barking companion fled into the depth of his yard and Farna chased enthusiastically after him.

Dogs that are trained specifically for protection or attack work can become over-aggressive. Muzzles are a humane way to keep this behavior under control.

Actually, a family dog is supposed to defend his territory and it would have been understandable if he had chased Farna away since she had no business in his yard.

Another of our dogs, Lady, once had her triumph as well. One day, a friend and I were standing and talking a few yards away from the garden gate of a mansion when the resident dog returned from an outing. Cautiously he crept in a crouch to his gate, shot through it, and, once behind the fence, started the customary barking. Lady placed her front paws on the top of the low fence in order to observe the action from up high. As fast as lightning, the "brave defender" disappeared around the nearest corner of the house.

Behind a fence, a dog will often play the role of the "brave defender."  **Unrestrained, however, he may not act so intimidating.**

Perhaps it is not easy to understand, but we do not take much of a risk when we enter a property where the resident dog puts on a wild performance at the fence. However, if he barks in a controlled and threatening manner or behaves calmly, we should be careful! It is possible that he will greet us with

The presence of dogs, even friendly dogs, in your home or yard will make intruders think twice about choosing it for a target.

friendliness, but it is also possible that he will give us a lesson we won't forget. Dog experts are attuned to the fine nuances in canine behavior that allow them to draw conclusions as to the dogs' good or evil intentions.

Taking a walk while on vacation, I saw a most beautiful German Shepherd Dog standing in a yard a few feet inside the gate. Of course, I had to talk to him and admire him. He looked friendly and interested and he wagged his tail. When I started to approach the gate, he suddenly changed into a sinister-looking defender, tense in a silently threatening posture. This was a dog as a dog should be: friendly to harmless people, ready to protect with suspicious ones. He did not need to put on a wild show.

DEFENSE OF THE HOME TERRITORY

In contrast to police dogs that take action only in the company of their handler and only upon his instructions, the guardian of the home is often left to his own devices, which places increased demands on his natural self-confidence. A dog possessing a good protection instinct and a steady temperament will, when the time comes, know how to perform his job as guard dog even without special training.

For other dogs, it is advisable to bolster their instinctive protective behavior by providing them with opportunities to try out this instinct in real life. Our dog is to practice defense, not to attack, as is too often assumed. Experience must teach him that his

defensive actions are respected. This strengthens his backbone and thus builds his confidence. We would like our dog to protect our home by barring an intruder's way, either through barking threateningly while standing directly in front of him or by growling. This is the ideal behavior that we cannot really expect from all dogs, but it should be included in training as one of our goals.

When the dog is still a puppy we take him along whenever we answer the

A wire crate provides a dog with safe confinement while allowing him to see what's going on around him.

Dogs are naturally protective of their home territory; however, they do need special training if they are to work as guard dogs.

doorbell. We want to familiarize him with this type of situation from the very beginning. While the door is still closed, the pup will probably bark. As soon as we open the door, the barking will usually stop. Since there are no aggressive intentions, this new and interesting situation totally captures his attention.

Normally, young dogs will behave neutrally toward visitors as long as their urge to defend their territory has not yet been awakened. However, if a puppy displays aggressiveness, then interacting with visitors excites him more than it is worth. In this case, we must practice introducing the pup to new people and practice having him interact with guests until he can do so calmly.

In this first phase of training it is our goal to relieve our dog's insecurity toward strangers that come to the house. To help with such exercises, we need to enlist the aid of some people who know how to interact with dogs and do not allow themselves to be easily intimidated.

Furthermore, the dog must have these early experiences at the place where we will later put him to work if he is to be a guard dog. For instance, we had a front yard where the dog was supposed to later perform his guard duty. The helper would ring the bell and enter the yard right away. At the same time my dog and I would step out of the house and approach the visitor.

Some pups would run immediately toward the helper and stop a short distance in front of him without barking. Others would rush off and bark at him. There were also some who stuck by their owner's heels, some barking, some silent. Every time this exercise was repeated, their behavior improved.

The helper should do nothing but stop and stand still. He must not allow himself to be intimidated, nor should he attack. Either could induce the dog to attack. If the dog should circle him, he must follow this movement in order to maintain the "in front" position. Many dogs would nip if they could catch someone from the rear.

With overly aggressive dogs, we work with muzzles. Muzzles are a good means to decrease excessive aggressiveness. A muzzle is in no way an instrument of torture as some sentimental people are inclined to believe. If used short-term in tricky situations, a dog will

For dogs that are scared or in pain, a muzzle is a safety precaution. It can protect the dog and any people nearby, and is safe and easy to use. Photo courtesy of Four Paws.

forget that he is wearing one. Attacking harmless people is not a heroic deed. These dogs possess a pronounced instinct to defend their territory; an instinct that is, of course, desirable. What is lacking is the necessary self-confidence to know when to differentiate between a true threat and a perceived threat.

The more self-confidence our young dog is able to develop when confronting strangers, the better he will be able to later master his task as guard dog.

We cannot expect any protective behavior until his instinct to defend has been awakened. This may take some time, depending on the individual dog, so patience is necessary.

As soon as the young dog demonstrates the behavior we desire, we stay further and further away from the place of action. When things work without our involvement, we practice during different times of the day and eventually in darkness.

Of course, this training does not go as quickly as you can read these suggestions. The development proceeds quite slowly, step by step, and can take many months. Only after the dog has fully matured can we expect him to fully exert himself.

OUR WATCHDOG

Dogs are very light sleepers. Even dogs that are not given to barking are immediately alert when they hear an unusual noise. Any unusual noise, especially at night, is disquieting for our dog just as it is for us. He will report the noise as long as his worry does not turn into fear. If he is afraid, he will stay as quiet as a mouse—just as we would—unless he feels immediately threatened.

Most people think that dogs of the nervous type who bark at the slightest provocation make the best watchdogs. According to our experiences that is not true at all. For many years we owned four German Shepherd Dogs, three of which slept in kennels at night. When Dally and Farna happened to bark at night, we knew for sure that some sort of animal had shown up: a hedgehog, a rabbit, a cat, etc.

Dogs are natural watchdogs, as they immediately become alert at any unusual noises. The German Shepherd Dog is a popular watchdog breed.

One night, however, only Filou barked; not a sound out of the other two. He was not barking excitedly, but low and threateningly. My husband went to check what was going on, but did not see anything. The next morning we found out that the neighbor's house, about 45 yards away, had been broken into.

Those looking for a good watchdog must station their friend according to his temperament. He should be housed at night in such a way that, if danger should arise,

he will neither be afraid and hide nor feel so secure that he, in all innocence, won't make a sound. It is the mental state between fear and superiority that brings about the desired state of mind. We just have to work by trial and error. After all, our watchdog is only to report what is unusual and not take sleep-disturbing note of familiar noises. Thus, we may have to move his sleeping place. All too "watchful" dogs should sleep closer to their master — all too indifferent ones farther away from him. It

may also happen that we have to make adjustments as the dog matures.

Much more could be said on the topic of training dogs; however, you have been supplied with the basics. Each dog is different and so is each handler. Again and again we encounter new situations and problems, so it is impossible to anticipate every circumstance. However, you should be fine if you follow the general guidelines and try to understand and communicate with your dog.

 Dogs have a comforting presence—this therapy Golden helps a young friend relax during a visit to the doctor.

PROBLEMS WITH THE ENVIRONMENT

It is imperative that a dog learns to walk politely on a leash and behave well amidst everyday distractions while he is still young.

◄◄ **Dogs and children are a natural (but potentially messy) combination!**

Introducing our young puppy to our world, a world that is alien to the canine species, should happen cautiously and always under the supervision and protection of someone he knows. We should carefully observe his responses to the various stimuli that he experiences on our outings. The youngster's responses tell us a lot about his temperament, his willingness to take risks, and the state of his nerves.

For example, if the puppy should shy from some object when out walking with us—a strangely shaped tree stump, perhaps, or something that moves in a strange way or makes unusual noises—then we should calmly approach the object and, talking in a soothing voice, make it clear to the youngster that there is nothing to be afraid of.

As the dog continues to encounter new and different things, he will behave better and learn how to deal with them. He will approach the objects more readily, examine them more closely, and bark less. Such successful experiences are absolutely necessary for proper development.

We may, of course, intentionally arrange for such stimulus situations, and we should do so often. Towels fluttering in the wind, rattling pot lids, flashing lights, and other everyday things around the house will do just fine.

When they are between three and five months old, puppies should be especially curious and still very unabashed. They should totally trust and rely on their "guardian angels"—their handlers. It is amazing how well most of pups react to "stimulus situations," provided they are raised properly.

TRAFFIC SAFETY

The sights and sounds of traffic are something else with which we should cautiously familiarize our puppy while he is still young. After we have prepared him by walking on less busy streets, we take him to busier streets. However, we should only do this if the youngster is totally comfortable, that is, he walks in a relaxed manner on a loose leash. As long as he keeps

If you own a dog, you have to worry about ticks. One preventive measure is to have the dog wear a collar that contains a compound that stops ticks from feeding on dogs by paralyzing their mouth parts so they can't attach to a dog's skin. Consider using it as another weapon in your tick-control arsenal. Photo courtesy of Francodex.

It's not always easy to get your dog to take a bath, but bath time seems like fun for this Boxer and his young campanion.

"pulling," he is not yet secure with the situation and it is best to just take it slow.

CAR RIDES

Even if we have no intentions of taking our dog on frequent car rides, we should still accustom him to our car while he is young; it is simply a part of the training program. There will be times when we will have to take him in the car to the veterinarian, to the training classes to large parks and on vacation with us.

A car ride is totally foreign experience for our dog. It is certainly not natural that suddenly the "house" begins to shake! His first reaction will depend on his temperament. Calm, bold types are frequently excited at first, which is usually misinterpreted as enthusiasm. In reality, it expresses worry. Shy dogs often behave with unnatural calm. Dogs that are fearful and easily excitable become confused and worried.

If the dog's mouth is clamped tightly shut, it is a sign that he is worried or even afraid. Only when he is able to

It's a good idea to bring a supply of your dog's regular food along when you travel. That way you know your dog will be getting a complete and balanced food whenever you're on the road. Photo courtesy of Nature's Recipe Pet Foods.

keep his mouth slightly open can we be sure that he is no longer insecure. Some dogs take longer than others to become accustomed to car travel—it depends on his character.

You should invest in a fiberglass traveling crate, which will provide your dog with a safe place to ride. Accustom him to the crate before putting him in the crate in the car and driving off. If you don't want to use a crate, keep your dog in the very back of the vehicle, separated from you by a special screen, or in the back seat. He could cause an accident jumping from seat to seat in the car.

In the long run, most dogs are enthusiastic car travelers, provided they are accustomed to this adventure carefully at an early age. If, despite our caution, our dog should become carsick, we can administer a medication to prevent motion sickness. The dosage is determined by the weight—consult with your veterinarian.

NERVOUS RESPONSES

Dogs that bark excitely do not have steady nerves and their barking is an indication of their insecurity. They are not really aggressive, they are only "carrying on" in a nervous response. Handlers should recognize this type of response and react by trying to calm their dogs with soothing words.

There is a temptation to treat such nervous dogs very delicately. This is absolutely wrong. On the contrary, we must give them many opportunities to interact with their surroundings. In doing so, we should let things run their

"Let's go for a ride!" You should take your dog for short trips in the car to help him get used to traveling. Invest in a travel crate—it's the safest way for your dog to ride.

natural course as much as possible and assist the puppy only with calming words in a deep, gentle voice. Handled in this way, he will become progressively quieter with each occurrence and will approach questionable objects a little bit closer each time. As this happens, his temperament will develop and become more stable. His stimulus threshold will be heightened, which is a very desirable development.

Nervous dogs make greater demands on the trainer's skill and patience. A novice in dog handling will have a considerably easier time with a calm dog.

An alert Rottweiler stands watch over his territory. ➡

The Border Collie is a breed known for its keen intelligence and high degree of trainability. This dog stares intently at something that has caught his attention.

SUGGESTED READING

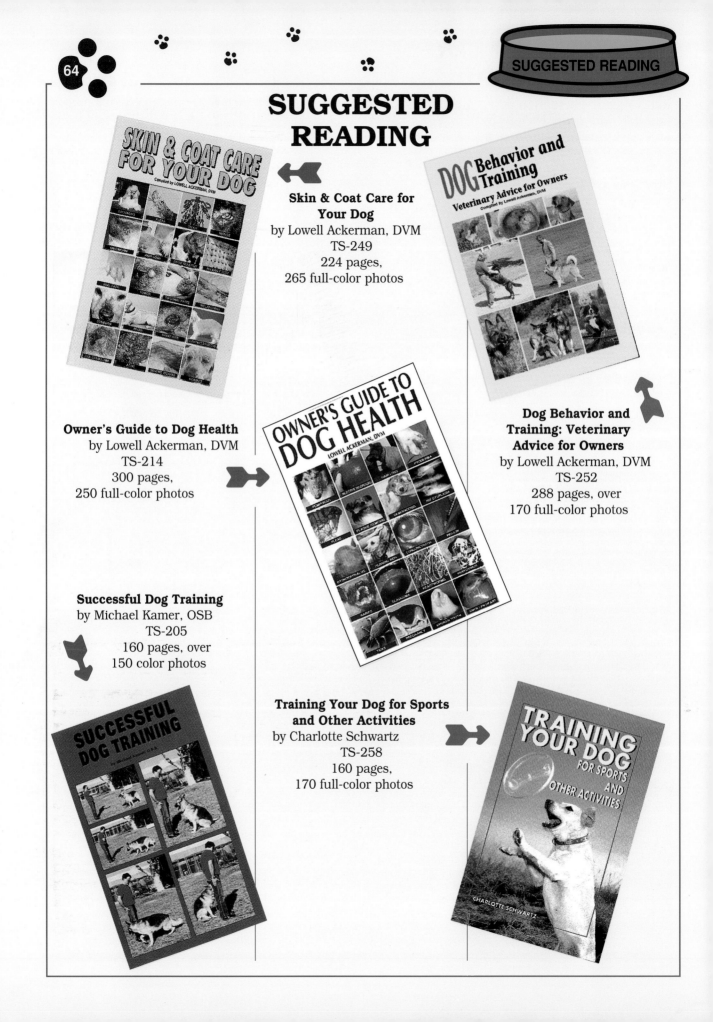

Skin & Coat Care for Your Dog
by Lowell Ackerman, DVM
TS-249
224 pages,
265 full-color photos

Dog Behavior and Training: Veterinary Advice for Owners
by Lowell Ackerman, DVM
TS-252
288 pages, over
170 full-color photos

Owner's Guide to Dog Health
by Lowell Ackerman, DVM
TS-214
300 pages,
250 full-color photos

Successful Dog Training
by Michael Kamer, OSB
TS-205
160 pages, over
150 color photos

Training Your Dog for Sports and Other Activities
by Charlotte Schwartz
TS-258
160 pages,
170 full-color photos